Welcome!

Introducing Pompey Poems - a playful collection of stories about the charming creatures who roam the streets, skies, and shores of Portsmouth. Each poem introduces a new character from a different part of our vibrant city.

You'll meet animals that dream big, like Harry the Heron, who secretly wishes for a modelling career, and the ever-so-proud Don Swan, the self-proclaimed king of Canoe Lake.

There's also characters from beyond Portsmouth, like the Hayling Hippo, who reminds us all to love ourselves just as we are!

Author & Artist

Michael Jon Ward is a Welshman who moved to Southsea in 2002 to attend Portsmouth University. After graduating, he founded Tidy Design and started a family, making the South Coast his home. With a deep love for fine art and creative writing, Mike blends his passion for storytelling and illustration in Pompey Poems.

Offering free stories on his website, Mike was pleasantly surprised when he was contacted by a local school:

"I came across your poem The Southsea Seagull and shared it with my Year 6 children, and they absolutely loved it. They loved the references to Southsea — they couldn't believe someone had written about the seagulls in Southsea and were very much in agreement that they always know where the chips are. Their love and happiness from this poem has made me get in touch."

This inspired him to write and illustrate even more playful stories for kids to enjoy!

STORIES

The Southsea Seagull

Albert Road Toad

The Gosport Gannet

Colin The Canoe Lake Crab

Solent Seal

Cat on the Common

Don Swan

The Hayling Hippo

Harry the Heron

The Palmerston Pigeon

The Fratton Falcon

Plus there is room for you to create your own Local Legend

Now, let's take a stroll through these pages and discover the delightful creatures that call Pompey home.

The Southsea Seagull

High above the stones and shells

High above the pier

Looking down for food to eat

You'll know when he is near

He really does love chunky chips

And he loves the batter

There is no diet on his mind

He's happy getting fatter

Pigeons, crows and other gulls

They all know the score

This seagull is relentless

Always wanting more

With a big fat bloated belly
He struggles to fly far
A giant poop from high above
Destroys a nice clean car

You're kidding me, hungry again
Will he ever stop!
If that belly got much bigger
This gull would surely pop

Daily trips to Southsea Beach
Looking out for food
Canoe Lake, the castle too
Depending on his mood

Anywhere you'd eat your chips
This is where he'll be
Waiting for a chip to fall
A chip to eat for tea

This gulls eyesight is not great
Children may well shriek
Small fingers often look like chips
And end up in his beak

There is no cloud above you
There is no eclipse
It's just The Southsea Seagull
Staring at your chips

ALBERT ROAD TOAD

On Albert Road
Amidst the moon light
Lives a sneaky toad
Who comes out at night

With warty brown skin
And a hop in his stride
The Albert Road Toad
Is so full of pride

Through alleys he hops
In search of some fun
This toad knows the spots
To shake his big bum

He croaks with delight
At the pubs and the bars
Avoiding the feet
And noise of the cars

He loves going out
And the bustling crowd
Sometimes he's shy
Sometimes he's loud

With a flick of his tongue
And a wink of his eyes
The Albert Road Toad
Orders drinks with some flies

Strutting and leaping

Warts big and alarming

His favourite line:

"Could I be your Prince Charming?"

But now it is late

He looks at his phone

With a wink and a grin

It's time to hop home

THE GOSPORT
GANNET

By the Gosport shores
Lives a bird you will see
Known for its appetite
He's called the "Big G"

Other birds watch him
With eyes wide open
The Gosport Gannet
He's so well-spoken

He tries to fit in
But it's never enough
For the gannet's hunger
Makes friendships tough

Yet he keeps on trying
To meet other birds
Offering kindness
And sharing wise words

A gold chain gleams
As he dives to the sea
Searching for fish
To eat for his tea

Flying with flair
In stylish attire
The Big G's fashion
Is much to admire

But he's more than bling
More than just words
He is an inspiration
To so many birds

He's chasing a dream
To live in the city
No cliff tops, no colony
No noisy committee

He wanted adventure
His life to be merry
Weekends in Gunwharf
Trips on the ferry

Yes, he is different

He's not like the rest

But this doesn't matter

We think he's the best

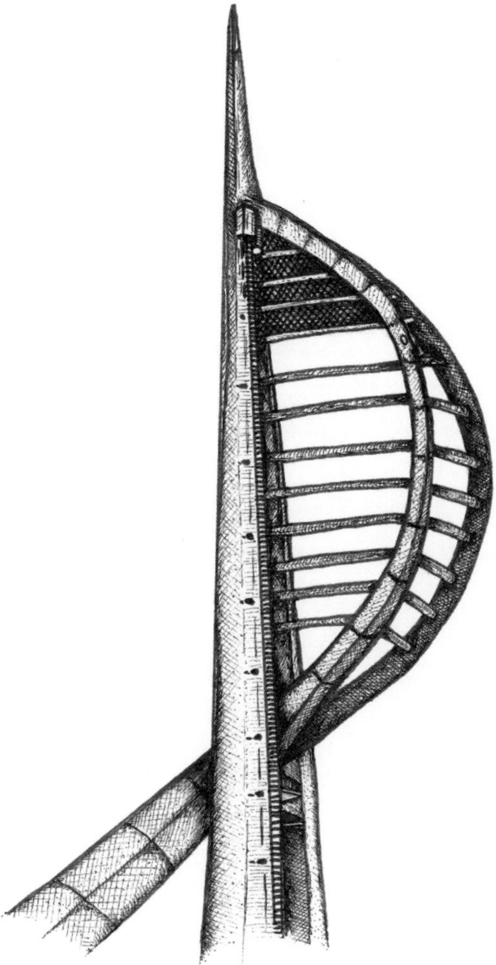

Colin The Canoe Lake Crab

Deep in Canoe Lake
Where the swan boats glide
Lives Colin the crab
In his secret hide

He is very old
Bigger than a duck
But to catch Colin
You'll need more than luck

A beast of a crab
With a shell so grand
Claws strong and mighty
Bigger than your hand

He scuttles and hides

In places unknown

Master of disguise

How big he has grown

With a sideways walk

He likes to explore

And eat BIG dinners

He always wants more

Colin's prehistoric

From a time long gone

His favourite dinner

Is Canoe Lake swan

Colin's so clever

He speaks duck, "quack quack"

Ducks are so tasty

And make a nice snack

So… have you seen him?

Please make no mistake

A big scary monster

Lives in Canoe Lake

Solent Seal

Out on the Solent
A cheeky young seal
Chasing the fish
For a fun, fresh meal

Busy and active
He stays out of sight
By Southsea Castle
From dawn until night

A big chunky seal
Proud of his blubber
Asks "why so much litter?
Plastics and rubber!"

His home is the solent

He wants it kept clean

Leaving your rubbish

Is selfish and mean

"What is that floating?"

It makes him so sad

"A plastic bottle!"

It's making him mad!

An angry seal

Can be quite scary

A mouth full of teeth

Cheeks very hairy

So next time you visit

The beach or the sea

Remember the seal

And keep it trash-free

A clean, happy shore

Joy for all creatures

A simple message:

"Protect our beaches!"

CAT ON THE COMMON

On Southsea Common

Lives a sneaky cat

Who causes trouble

Just imagine that!

She prowls through the grass

With an evil grin

Hiding in bushes

Waiting to begin

Targeting walkers

With dogs big or small

They run and they bark

"Missed me!" she will call

Leaps into the path
Of runners in stride
Making them startle
Then runs off to hide

This cat loves chaos
The fun and the thrill
Playing her pranks
With plenty of skill

Her favourite game
Is 'under your feet'
Pretending to be
So gentle and sweet

Then without warning

Not making a sound

She'll pounce on your toes

And chase you around

Some say she's a myth

And not really there

But try telling that

To the people she scares

Don Swan

Godfather to birds
With feathers so sleek
He commands respect
From every beak

A swan of stature
He is quite a sight
Grunting like a boss
From morning till night

He rules Canoe Lake
With an iron wing
To all other birds
This swan is a king

He does love his food
Fresh with some flavour
You pay him in snacks
Don gives a favour

Gifting protection
To birds on the lake
Payment is simple
Bread, crisps or cake

A giant crab lurks
In his armoured shell
He is the reason
the birds pay so well

Don is a fixer

Confident and tall

Waddling around

He knows and sees all

There's peace on the lake

Everyone gets on

And this is because

The legend Don Swan

The Hayling Hippo

A mouth wide open

A belly so big

Happy and chubby

She laughs like a pig

The Hayling Hippo

Lives by the shore

With rough, tough skin

She always wants more

More salad, more veg

A big bag of chips

She waddles through town

With oversized hips

The Hayling Hippo
Her mouth open wide
There is no dentist
Who'd dare look inside

But this won't stop her
Cracking a smile
This hippo is cool
This hippo's got style

She's an outsider
With very tough skin
On Hayling Island
She tries to fit in

Wearing a sunhat
And shades on her snout
Down by the seaside
She waddles about

A local celeb
That doesn't quite blend
The Hayling Hippo
Your lovable friend

Harry the Heron

Southsea Rock Gardens
A fish-catchers dream
Harry the Heron
Perched by the stream

Silent and waiting
With a keen sharp eye
Hungry for dinner
No fish shall pass by

He's quick with his strike
And then quick to flee
Harry the Heron
was catching his tea

But deep down inside
He dreams of the day
When he'll walk the catwalk
And model away

Legs long and slender
With feathers so sleek
Harry the Heron
Hangs fish from his beak

Accessory mad
He soon strikes a pose
People are watching
In bird watching clothes

Sitting in silence

Binoculars out

Watching young Harry

Strutting about

Adored by many

He is quite a dish

Everyone loves him

Except for the fish

The Palmerston Pigeon

On Palmerston Road

It's quite a sight

Near the shops and pubs

A pigeon takes flight

With shiny blue feathers

And bright orange feet

The Palmerston Pigeon

Is who you will meet

Through crowds he weaves

A perfect landing

The Palmerston Pigeon

His chest expanding

Pigeons are social
They do like to talk
Well, it's more a "coo-coo"
They say when they walk

Yes they are vocal
And it's not all about food
Sometimes their fighting
Sometimes they're rude

With a flap of their wings
And a flick of their tail
They strut and they coo
Everyday without fail

The Palmerston Pigeon
The king of his road
A "coo-coo" so loud
Your ears will explode

Strutting and pacing
With pride in his stride
But what makes him happy
Is food by his side

His road, his rules
This is what he said:
"Give me some snacks
Or I'll poop on your head!"

The Fratton Falcon

At Portsmouth F.C
Where the fans roar loud
The Fratton Falcon
Soars over the crowd

With feathers so sleek
He joins in the cheer
Supporting his team
Year after year

The Pompey Peregrine
Swift, strong, and slick
A footballing bird
That moves very quick

Blink and you'll miss him
A talent so rare
In a Pompey blue shirt
He flies through the air

200 miles an hour
The speed of his dive
With the wind in his face
He feels so alive

Ready and focused
A championship dream
From high above Fratton
He cheers on his team

Triumphs or losses

He'll never depart

For Pompey lives on

In this falcons heart

LOCAL LEGEND

Portsmouth is full of untold stories. Think of a location and draw your very own Portsmouth creature.

Next...

Grab a pencil, crayons, or paints and let your imagination run wild! Once you've created your character, write a short story or poem about their adventures. Your Local Legend could be the next big star of Pompey!

What about the pier, who lives here?

There is also Portsmouth Cathedral…

The Queens Hotel...

And Southsea Castle

Make a list of your favorite local attractions and see if you can imagine the creatures that call them home.

Thank You

A huge thank you to those who purchase this book - I truly hope you enjoyed reading it. To my two boys, Isaac and Jamie, for always keeping me creative and motivated. Also a big thanks to my parents and a few close friends for their endless support, proof-reading, and feedback throughout the creation process.

Read More...

If you enjoyed Pompey Poems, you might also like my other stories, Tina The Christmas Turkey and Halloween Stories for Kids.

Be sure to check them out!

MJWard

Printed in Great Britain
by Amazon